SUPPERLOVE

David Bez of Pride Kitchen

SUPPERLOVE

Comfort bowls for
quick and nourishing suppers

quadrille

For my family

Publishing Director: Sarah Lavelle
Creative Director: Helen Lewis
Commissioning Editor: Céline Hughes
Designer and Photographer: David Bez
Production: Tom Moore, Vincent Smith

First published in 2017 by
Quadrille Publishing
Pentagon House
52–54 Southwark Street
London SE1 1UN
www.quadrille.co.uk

Quadrille is an imprint of Hardie Grant
www.hardiegrant.com.au

Cataloguing in Publication Data: a catalogue record for this
book is available from the British Library.

UK ISBN: 978 184949 964 4
US ISBN: 978 178713 049 4

Printed in China

CONTENTS

MY CAFÉ, MY FOOD
and the winter months

In 2010 I started getting interested in how to feed myself something healthier and tastier than what I could find either locally or in my office canteen. That need to control the ingredients on my plate and learn how to eat more unrefined foods, and more veggies in particular, led me on an incredible journey. My desire to make veggies more appealing and interesting made me become a very different person and a different professional in a very short time.

I've experimented extensively with lunch and then breakfast by creating hundreds of possible combinations. I tried again and again new ways to play with plants and I fell in love with them many times. In the book *Salad Love*, I fell in love with veggies mostly; in *Breakfast Love*, I rediscovered fruits.

My renewed love for plants was something I wanted to share – with my pictures, through social media, in my books – and I had a dream: to open a space where people could come and experience what it means to have a tasty, nourishing, filling and yet light lunch.

So I happened to bump into a little spot in Covent Garden, London and the magic of Neal's Yard captured my imagination; my dream felt ready to become real.

But before that, I had to find the money to make it come true. I looked to the web for crowd-funding, but mostly I looked at my origins, the beginning of my whole adventure. I needed £10,000 in order to fund my dream and that money came primarily from my family, friends and my incredibly loyal colleagues at the Discovery Channel. They are still the greatest supporters I have, as they saw the transformation of my life through the discovery of healthy food and witnessed my commitment to bringing that to the mainstream.

Now, looking at my customers smile while they enjoy their meals is so much more rewarding than just receiving a "like" on Instagram or Facebook. The real human interaction, the constant feedback, and the challenge of feeding my customers' taste buds, bellies and eyes (and not just their eyes any more), made me grow so much and learn so deeply about food, people and happiness.

The café opened in spring, so a long summer of salads and breakfasts kept all my customers happy and satisfied. But as soon as September, with its first chill, hit the city, I felt something had to change. Comfort food was going to be my next challenge; enough of cold salads.

At the same time, my love for plants grew even more and I decided to make plants the only choice. The café became vegan and I changed its name from SaladPride, my beginning, to Pride Kitchen.

COMFORT BOWLS
of nourishing grains and soups

I really like simple food that's full of flavour and as natural as can be. That's why I try to process the ingredients as little as possible. I investigated many culinary traditions to find their comfort food classics, looking for inspiration for dishes that are balanced and nutritious, something that can fill you without killing energy, something that can keep you sharp and energized but stilll give you that comforting, feel-good experience.

Back at the Discovery Channel, I remember my friend Elle wondering if I could serve what she called "wet hot salads", which I thought was a funny and quite bizarre idea at the time. But when I started this project, Elle's idea came back to me again and again. Initially I called them salad-soups, but the name didn't sound appealing. Then I explored the Asian tradition of ramen, pho and curries and their combinations of raw and cooked veggies, meats, eggs and carbs. This gave me the insight to rethink those "soupy salads".

Why not use veggies as noodles? Why not add more raw and fresh veggies instead of over-boiling them, like in a classic minestrone? I've always been a big fan of raw eating and I've always understood the nutritional value of fresh, raw veggies and the use of fermented foods. But the main question was, could you use these ingredients to make comfort food? Is it possible to have comfort food with fewer carbs, less dairy, fish or meat and more veggies, seeds, beans and herbs? I believe so.

I have divided the book into two chapters. The first covers all the weird and wonderful soups I came up with, and the second is filled with more substantial hot or warm bowls. There's nothing completely new or completely strange in this book, but it is packed with my incredibly extended research about what it means to have a nourishing and fulfilling supper and it will challenge your idea of what a soup or meal is.

ANATOMY OF A SOUP BOWL

When composing my soups, I divide it into different layers: a base, vegetables, proteins, toppings and some kind of broth or cream. These are the main ingredients, but as you will see, I often mess around with the formula. It's really up to you what you choose to put in it and to enjoy what you are eating. I like my bowl to be 20% base, 50% veggies, 25% protein, 5% toppings and herbs, plus the broth or the soup.

BASE

The base can be variable, from noodles or quinoa, but also filling veggies like cauliflower, courgettes [zucchini] and squash, to name a few.

VEGETABLES

The biggest part of my dinner is always the veggies. At least two vegetable portions are included in my supper bowl – either cooked or raw. This is a big change from conventional dinners based mainly on starch, fish or meat.

PROTEIN

Proteins are a very important part of my dinner; I like to add a handful of the protein I crave the most, but not just ham, beef, chicken, eggs or fish – it can be also yogurt, cheese, tofu, lentils, quinoa, nuts or seeds depending on your own dietary requirements and your tastes.

TOPPINGS

Toppings are what will boost the flavours and colours of your dinner bowl and add a special kick to it. I love to add fermented or pickled veggies like sauerkraut or olives, but toasted nuts and seeds are also great.

FRESH HERBS

I try to add a handful of fresh herbs like basil, chives or coriander [cilantro] – or even spring onions [scallions] – which give an amazing flavour boost.

BROTH OR CREAM

This is the element that flavours and binds together your soup. I make a distinction between two types: broths and creamy soups.

BROTHS AND CREAMS

When I started working on this book about dinner, I was keen to create something that could happily feed my customers in my café in the winter. I started questioning and researching what a soup is and what a broth is.

Everything starts from a broth. Of course, you can easily buy vegetable, fish, beef and chicken stock in supermarkets, but I prefer to make my own. I have a no-waste policy in my café and at home, too, so my vegetable broth is always created by boiling the off-cuts of my veggies, or the unused veggies of the day, with just a little bit of salt and dried herbs, like bay leaves, thyme, sage or rosemary. I often add extras, such as dried seaweed and/or miso paste to add flavour and saltiness. In fact, my favourite broth right now is the easiest ever – water, salt, dulse seaweed, miso paste, dried shiitake mushrooms. Boil and stir for 15 minutes. (See page 18.) That's it.

The same method applies for meat or fish broths. Take all the off-cuts of your meal and boil them – the longer the better. But I'm no bone-broth specialist; I prefer vegetable-based broths.

The other type of soup I favour is the creamy type, and these are a different story. I started by playing with coconut milk and adding different spices inspired by Thai and Indian cuisines, but I ended up preferring something lighter and less spicy – a sort of creamy broth.

I like to use very simple creams such as single [light] cream, rice or soy cream, or even cashew cream, with just a few spices added to it like salt, pepper, paprika, ginger and turmeric. I experimented by adding other veggies or juices, like squash, or beetroot [beet] juice.

I also like to make raw "broths/creams" that are ultimately mostly vegetable "smoothies".

BROTHS

VEGETABLE

1 cup water, 1 cup chopped raw vegetable off-cuts and scraps (no potatoes), ½ onion, 2 bay leaves. Boil in a pan for at least 1 hour, then strain.

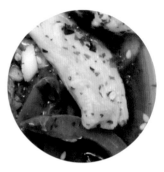

CHICKEN

1 chopped onion, 1 chopped carrot, a bunch each of fresh thyme and rosemary, all the bones from 1 roasted chicken, and enough water to cover everything in a pan. Boil for 1 hour, then strain and cool quickly.

BEEF

1 chopped onion, 1 chopped celery stick, a bunch of fresh sage, 1 garlic clove, a few bones from a joint of roast beef, and enough water to cover everything in a pan. Boil for 1 hour, then strain and cool quickly.

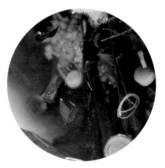

SEAWEED & MISO

A handful each of dried mushrooms and dulse seaweed, 1 cup water. Bring to the boil in a pan, boil for 20 minutes, then strain out just the mushrooms. Leave the seaweed and stir in 1 tbsp miso paste.

CREAMS

COCONUT CREAM

250 ml [1 cup] coconut cream, 250 ml [1 cup] boiling water, 1 tbsp ground turmeric, 1 tbsp cayenne pepper, salt and black pepper. Heat in a pan until hot.

CREAM & VEGETABLES

Heat up 250 ml [1 cup] single [light] cream in a pan. Add a handful of roasted or raw vegetables of your choice (beetroot [beet], carrot, [bell] pepper, artichoke, mushroom), 125 ml [½ cup] boiling water, salt and pepper, and blend.

RAW SMOOTHIE

Blend together 1 cup water, 1 cup chopped raw vegetables of your choice (tomato, carrot, celeriac, [bell] pepper, fennel), salt and pepper.

RAW CASHEW

Blend together 1 tsp extra virgin olive oil, 1 cup water, 2 tbsp cashew nuts (soaked overnight), a pinch of salt.

ANATOMY OF A NOURISHING BOWL

When composing my nourishing bowl, I divide it into different layers, just as I do with my soups: a base, vegetables, proteins, toppings and some kind of sauce, cream or dressing. These are the main ingredients, but as you will see, I often mess around with the formula. It's really up to you what you choose to put in it and to enjoy what you are eating. I like my bowl to be 20% base, 50% veggies, 25% protein, 5% toppings and herbs, plus the sauce or dressing.

BASE
The base can be variable, from noodles or pasta, to rice and buckwheat, but also filling veggies like sweet potato, cabbage and beetroot [beet], to name a few.

VEGETABLES
The biggest part of my dinner is always the veggies. At least two vegetable portions are included in my supper bowl – either cooked or raw. This is a big change from conventional dinners, based mainly on starch, fish or meat.

PROTEIN

Proteins are a very important part of my dinner. I like to add a handful of the protein I crave the most, but not just ham, beef, chicken, eggs or fish – it can be also yogurt, cheese, tofu, lentils, quinoa, nuts or seeds depending on your own dietary requirements and your tastes.

TOPPINGS

Toppings are what will boost the flavours and colours of your dinner bowl and add a special kick to it. I love to add fermented or pickled veggies like sauerkraut or olives, but toasted nuts and seeds are also great.

FRESH HERBS

I try to add a handful of fresh herbs like baby coriander [cilantro] to my dinner, which provide an amazing flavour boost.

SAUCE

This is the element that flavours and binds together your nourishing bowl. It can be a dressing, sauce, or hummus.

DRESSINGS AND SAUCES

When I think about how to dress my supper bowls, I first look at what kinds of ingredient I have, particularly what kind of base. Couscous, rice, barley, quinoa and grains often just need a nice dressing to give some extra flavour, while other bases like spaghetti, noodles, courgetti or kale often feel like they need something richer, creamier or saucier.

DRESSINGS

I have written a lot in the past about dressings, but more than ever I feel passionate about them, as they are where meals are made or ruined.

My rule for dressings is simple: 3 parts oil, 1 part acidity (like vinegar, soy sauce or citrus juice), 1 part creaminess (cream, tahini, yogurt or nut butter), 1 part sweetness (honey, maple syrup, dates or agave nectar), 1 part herbs or spices (mustard, thyme, basil, seaweed sprinkles, fennel, paprika, ginger, chilli, turmeric, and so on).

I rarely use more than 1 spice at a time, and never more than 2 – in order to taste a spice in your dressing, you need to focus on one and work around it. For me, smoked paprika works fantastically with extra virgin olive oil, cider vinegar, tahini and honey. Seaweed (like dulse) works super well with raw sesame oil, tamari soy sauce, and rice or date syrup. Play around with your spices. It's fun!

SAUCES

Sauces are more varied than dressings. They range from homemade sauces like pesto or tomato sauce, to dips like hummus or babaganoush, or even ketchup and barbecue sauce, all the way through to something as simple as yogurt. But I like to experiment by mixing things together. I create them from scratch, they are all unique and there is no set rule – just your imagination and taste.

DRESSINGS

CLASSIC ITALIAN

2 tbsp extra virgin olive oil, 1 tsp balsamic vinegar, a pinch of salt and pepper

TAMARI SOY SAUCE

1 tsp tamari soy sauce, 2 tbsp rapeseed oil

RAW NUT CREAM

Blend together 2 tbsp extra virgin olive oil, 2 tbsp cashew nuts, a pinch of salt, 1 tsp water and 1 tsp agave nectar

ENGLISH MUSTARD

2 tbsp extra virgin olive oil, 1 tbsp mayonnaise, 1 tsp English mustard, a pinch of salt

SAUCES

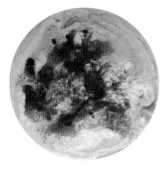

HUMMUS

2 tbsp extra virgin olive oil, 2 tbsp hummus, 1 tsp lemon juice, a pinch of salt and pepper, a couple of pinches of smoked paprika

CLASSIC PESTO

Blend together 2 tbsp extra virgin olive oil, a pinch of salt and pepper, a handful of fresh basil, 1 tbsp pine nuts, 1 tbsp parmesan cheese, ¼ garlic clove

SUN-DRIED TOMATO PESTO

Blend together 1 tsp sun-dried tomatoes, 2 tsp extra virgin olive oil, 1 tsp cider vinegar, a pinch of salt and pepper

LIGHT GUACAMOLE

Blend together ½ avocado, a handful of fresh herbs (e.g. basil, coriander, parsley), 1 tbsp lemon juice, 1 tsp olive oil

1. BASES

The base of a supper is normally something like pasta or rice – a carbohydrate that is filling and starchy. But it is my intention to keep my carb intake quite low and minimize the use of gluten as much as possible, as I find it hard to digest. So I have lowered the carbohydrate content down to about 20% in my bowls.

I did still start from the usual carbs: rice, noodles, pasta, couscous and other cereals like barley and spelt. After a while I started introducing other gluten-free ones like quinoa, buckwheat, millet, amaranth and corn. I find those much easier on my tummy. I then played around with replacing spaghetti with courgetti and other spiralized vegetables, such as carrots or squash, or even beetroot or sweet potatoes. Cucumbers are really good spiralized – they even look like noodles. If you're not familiar with spiralized veg, just buy a spiralizer or julienne peeler and make them yourself; you'll see how good they are.

Another vegetable trick that's popular right now is cauliflower "rice". You take a bunch of raw cauliflower florets and pulse them in your blender or food processor until they resemble couscous. You can eat the "rice" raw, or boil it for a minute, or steam it slightly to make it softer. What you end up with is a replacement for couscous or rice that is still filling but rich in nutrients. You can also try this trick with beetroot – it looks very good and it's so rich in nutrients!

I also use as a base leaves like cabbage, kale, spinach, chard, pak choi and so on. All these veggies can be eaten raw, or massaged a bit with lemon juice to make them softer, or even lightly steamed, or stir-fried in a wok.

2. VEGETABLES

Vegetables are at the core of all my dishes. There's so much you can do with them with just some very simple cooking. I don't like to complicate things too much and I like to treat the vegetables in such a way that I can actually taste all the flavour. My preferred way of using them is by chopping them in a pretty way, or spiralizing them, or just shaving them into ribbons and leaving them fresh and raw. My second favourite way is to roast them in the oven which is very easy (see page 31). Sometimes I steam them, but I rarely fry them. Now and then I stir-fry them extremely briefly, as I like to keep them crunchy.

It's important that the vegetables get a chance to shine, so I never have more than two or three of them at a time in my soups and bowls.

My favourite vegetables to use raw are cucumbers, [bell] peppers, tomatoes, red onions, carrots, celery, courgettes [zucchini], radishes, beetroots [beets], cauliflower, broccoli, fennel, parsnip, asparagus, green beans and shallots.

My favourite vegetables to steam are butternut squash, artichokes, sweet potatoes, broccoli, asparagus, green beans, peas, Jerusalem artichokes and new potatoes.

My favourite vegetables to roast are [bell] peppers, butternut squash, onions, artichokes, sweet potatoes, broccoli, aubergines [eggplant], asparagus, green beans, peas, pumpkin, Jerusalem artichokes, new potatoes and shallots.

ROASTING

Roasting is by far my favourite way to cook vegetables, not just because steaming doesn't provide much flavour, but also because roasting is so straightforward.

To roast, just wash and chop the vegetables, if necessary. I tend to chop them roughly, and not too small or too big. Try to chop veg in evenly sized pieces so that they all roast at the same rate. Drizzle with some olive oil, season them and add a sprinkle of spice or flavouring of your choice if you like (e.g. rosemary, thyme, paprika, chilli, or tamari soy sauce, which is fantastic with mushrooms). Even just oil and salt will do the job. Chuck them into a roasting pan and roast in a hot oven (about 180°C/350°F) for about 30 minutes. If you've chopped the veg small, it might not even take that long.

While you're waiting, just chill or prepare the rest of your supper bowl.

SPIRALIZING

I've always loved playing with the shapes and presentation of vegetables so that they look more interesting on my plate. It's also a way to challenge our perceived dislike of something and to encourage us to eat with our eyes.

That's why I started changing the appearance of vegetables, first with just a potato peeler, and then a julienne peeler and so on, until I discovered the spiralizer. I love it! It's such a beautiful way to present food. I find it so elegant. But it also reminds me of spaghetti – and then memories of my childhood flood back.

I like to use the spiralizer on courgettes [zucchini], cucumber, squash, sweet potato, celeriac, apples, beetroot [beet], big carrots, parsnips and many more.

After spiralizing, I usually leave the vegetables raw – for example with courgettes or cucumber. However, sometimes I steam or stir-fry them.

It is possible to buy pre-spiralized veggies in some supermarkets, but buying a spiralizer is much more worthwhile, in my opinion.

3. PROTEIN

Protein is a very important part of my dinner, but it would never take up more than 25% of my plate, and I always rotate the types I eat. Sometimes I eat meat or fish (about once a week), but most of my meals feature nuts, beans, cheese or eggs. I like to stock up on vegetable proteins.

I only eat organic and free-range meat, and sustainably sourced and wild fish. Farmed fish is not very natural and it's questionable whether it's healthy. It doesn't appear to be a fair industry, so I would mostly stay away from it. However, I have heard good things about tilapia and hydroponic systems in which a cycle of fish sustains and feeds plants, and vice versa.

Mostly my supper bowl is less rich in protein than other people's might be, but I keep my protein choices pretty varied in order to consume as wide a range of protein types as possible.

Depending on your dietary requirements and your taste, you can get your protein from meat, seafood (e.g. cod , tuna, crab, sole, haddock, herring, lobster, mackerel, prawns [shrimp], salmon, sardines, scallops, seabass, trout, squid, octopus), eggs, cheese (e.g. mozzarella, ricotta, parmesan, brie, cottage cheese, goats' cheese, cheddar, gorgonzola, blue cheese, halloumi, gouda, manchego and so on), pulses (e.g. edamame beans and tofu, lentils, pinto, kidney or black/carlin beans, broad [fava] beans, mung beans, chickpeas, peas and so on), grains (quinoa, wheat, couscous, rice, amaranth, barley, rye, oats, buckwheat), or even nuts and seeds (hemp seeds, almonds, Brazil nuts, hazelnuts, walnuts, cashew nuts, pine nuts, pistachios, pumpkin seeds, sesame seeds).

I love eggs, and my top way to eat them is soft-boiled. This is my technique for soft-boiling them but this is a personal preference so stick with your way if you have one!

Fill a small, deep saucepan with water and bring to the boil. Carefully place the egg in the boiling water and leave to boil over a medium heat for 6–7 minutes. Now drain the water and transfer the egg to a little bowl filled with ice to prevent the egg from cooking any further. After a few minutes, peel the egg.

When it comes to beans, I don't recommend canned beans at all. It is healthier and tastier to cook beans yourself from raw. You will need to soak them overnight before cooking them, so get into a routine of soaking the necessary ingredients in a large bowl of cold water the night before your planned supper bowl. This includes nuts (especially almonds and cashews), grains and pulses like chickpeas, beans, red, wild and brown rice, spelt, barley and much more. Soaking them will help digestion and make the cooking time quicker the following day.

4. HERBS AND CRESSES

I always try to add a handful of fresh herbs to my salads.
They are an essential part of my recipes, adding a fresh, intense
flavour, burst of colour and contrasting taste to a supper bowl.
I recommend buying pots of fresh herbs and growing them on
a windowsill at home. They look great and last a long time!

Recently I discovered microgreens and cresses. Every herb we
know can be grown in baby versions and carry so much flavour
that you won't believe you hadn't known about them sooner. And
you can grow these at home, too! You'll soon discover more and
more interesting combinations and flavours, like baby radish, baby
fennel, sweet pea or red amaranth.

5. TOPPINGS

Toppings are a fantastic addition to soups or nourishing bowls;
they are that extra kick that will give your dish an amazing lift.

Normally I add seeds or nuts, and toasting them first will give an
added intensity of flavour.

I also love to add olives or other pickled or preserved vegetables
like capers, onions, radishes and so on.

Recently I fell in love with fermented foods, such as krauts and
kimchi. These ingredients are so incredibly tasty but they are also
probiotics which means that they are beneficial to gut health.

PICKLES

You can pickle pretty much any vegetables to make them tasty and keep well – radish, carrot, beetroot [beet], cucumber.

Certain veggies will be enhanced by blanching them first, e.g. beetroot, Brussels sprouts, carrots, ginger, green beans and [bell] peppers. Don't worry about blanching cucumbers or tomatoes.

I always add dry or fresh flavourings, but not too many. Just one dominant herb or spice will enhance the flavour of the veggie. My favourites are bay leaves, cumin, dill and mustard seeds, turmeric, garlic, oregano, thyme, and coriander, cardamom, caraway and fennel seeds. The radish pictured above is pickled with fresh coriander [cilantro] and coriander seeds.

To make my sweet and sour brine:
Combine 3 cups cider vinegar, 3 cups water, 2 tbsp sea salt and 2 tbsp sugar in a large pan. Bring to the boil and stir until the salt and sugar have dissolved. Then boil for 2 minutes. Remove from the heat.

Put your choice of sliced raw veg in sterilized jars and cover them completely with brine, up to 1 cm [½ in] away from the rim. Discard any leftover brine. Place the lids on the jars and refrigerate for at least 24 hours before serving.

Pickles will keep in the refrigerator for up to 1 month.

FERMENTING

I've never been a huge fan of sauerkraut and I barely knew what fermented foods were until a few years ago when my wife gifted me a fermentation class. The teacher, Anna Drozdova, was great, super passionate and knowledgeable about the benefits and practices of preserving food that way. Since then, I have worked with her to develop crazy new flavours for my cafés and I have begun to understand and appreciate that particular sour flavour and smell – from foods like sauerkraut and kimchi, to drinks like kefir and kombucha and more, from the importance of fermentation in bread like sourdough to fermented nut "cheeses".

I started experimenting and now my menus always include fermented foods and drinks – kombucha and cashew "cheeses", sauerkraut and fermented carrots and cauliflowers… I love them all.

There is a problem with fermentation, though. It's almost impossible to find good fermented food off the shelf in supermarkets; fermenting needs care. You must find a local artisan at your farmers' market or you have to make it yourself, but it's worth doing.

THE BASICS OF SAUERKRAUT

Trim off all the wilted or damaged leaves from a head of cabbage and cut out the core. Now weigh the cabbage to determine how much salt you will need later. The ratio is 1 tbsp salt per 1 kg [2¼ lb] cleaned and cored cabbage. Shred or julienne the cabbage and put in a mixing bowl. Add the correct amount of salt and, using your hands, massage the cabbage to release the juices. The salt draws water out of the cabbage and helps create the brine in which the cabbage can ferment and sour without rotting. The salt also has the effect of keeping the cabbage crunchy by inhibiting organisms and enzymes that soften it. If not enough water is released, redistribute the salt as much as you can and leave the cabbage to sit for 30 minutes–3 hours. To check if there is enough juice, squeeze a handful of the cabbage – you should see juice dripping off and a small pool of it should be visible at the bottom of the bowl. If there is still not enough juice, massage the cabbage a bit more and leave for another hour or so.

You can now pack the cabbage. Use a sterilized jar and add a little cabbage at a time. Tamp it down with a kitchen utensil like a rolling pin; this helps to pack the ingredients tightly, increasing the brine production and forcing the oxygen out of the jar. Make sure that all the bits of ingredients are well under the brine, as contact with air might make them rot and go mouldy. When you pack the jar, leave about 5 cm [2 in] free below the rim to allow for the juice to rise without spilling over. Close the lid, but it should not be airtight; if there is a rubber washer on the lid, just close the lid without using the washer to prevent the built-up CO_2 from spitting in your face when you open the jar.

Place the jar in an unobtrusive and preferably dark corner of the kitchen (I cover the jar lightly with a towel) where it won't be in anyone's way but where you will not forget about it. Leave it to ferment at room temperature. Check the sauerkraut daily to make sure it is still submerged or floating in brine. Generally, on the second or third day, you will see the brine rise to the top, then later it will go down again. You might see some white bubbly scum forming at the top of the jar. Just skim it off and don't worry if you leave some behind; this is the result of contact with the air and is a normal part of the fermenting process. Rinse the lid if necessary.

Always remember to keep the ingredients well under or floating in brine. After the first 5 or 6 days the activity will be less pronounced, so you can check your ferment every other day instead of daily. Ferment the kraut at room temperature for around 20–25 days so that all the strains of beneficial bacteria have a chance to form. Some people leave it to ferment even longer, for a few months. The longer it ferments, the tastier it becomes, but it is up to you and I encourage you to start tasting your ferment on day 3 so you know how the taste develops with time. Check the kraut regularly to make sure the cabbage is submerged under brine, open the jar slightly to release some air pressure that might build up (this process is known as burping). If you see that the cabbage is dry on the top and the brine is well below, then press down the cabbage using your fist until the brine comes on top. When the sauerkraut is ready, store the jar in a cool place like a pantry or fridge to slow down the fermentation process. Remember that the fermentation process is still going on even in the fridge, but just much slower.

Sauerkraut generally keeps well in the fridge for up to a year. At some point it might start losing flavour and become soft and unpalatable – this is when the bacteria is dying out.

SPICY RED SAUERKRAUT

1 kg [2¼ lb] red cabbage
1 lime
4–5 cm [2 in] fresh ginger
4–5 garlic cloves
1–2 tsp chilli flakes
unrefined sea salt (follow the instructions
  on page 41)

TURMERIC & MUSTARD SAUERKRAUT

1 kg [2¼ lb] white cabbage
2–3 tsp ground turmeric
1 tbsp yellow/brown mustard seeds
unrefined sea salt (follow the instructions
  on page 41)

FERMENTED CARROT & CARDAMOM

1 kg [2¼ lb] carrots
1–1½ tbsp ground cardamom
2½ tbsp unrefined sea salt

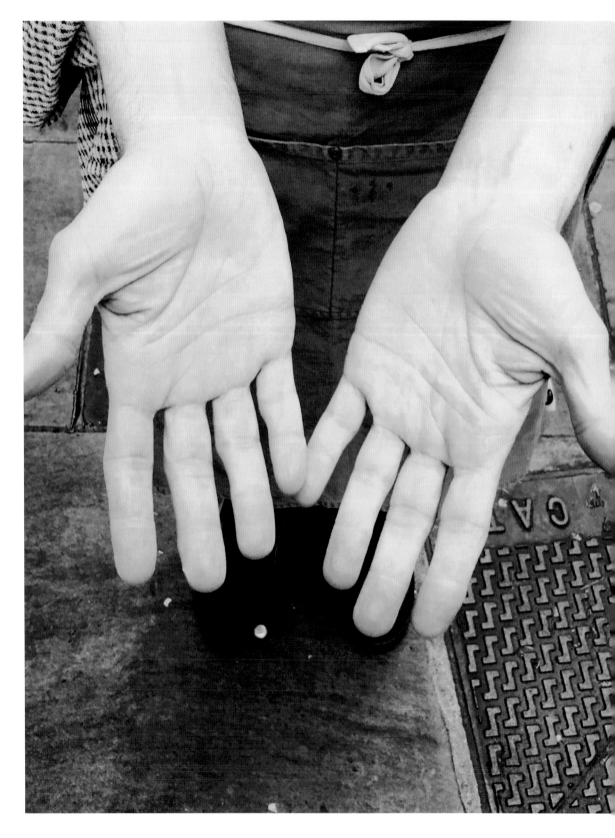

MY CONCLUSION

I wrote this book because I wanted to explore a simple yet satisfying way to get more vegetables into my dinner and my customers' dinners.

I decided to veer away from classic soups with lots of ingredients, overcooked for hours or blended together, because I like to have different consistencies and textures in my meal. I feel like I have found a really interesting way to eat comforting and warm food, rich in flavour, texture and also very rich in nutrients – from vitamins to proteins and all the minerals in between. I also tried to create something that does not require too much preparation, that's simple and that does not require amazing culinary skills. I also wanted it to be formulaic, as it is in my previous books, so that it can become the base for hundreds more creations.

Most of all, I tried to transform my dinners so that they became satisfying, nourishing and very tasty, but also comforting and relevant. I came across some weird and wonderful combinations – even some amusing ones – but overall I found that dinner can be rich and flavourful even with fewer carbohydrates and less meat. This, to me, is a gift.

Reducing meat consumption was crucial for me, and it became such a great decision especially after opening a plant-based café in central London. Eating plant-based food makes me happier and much better off in terms of energy, attention and digestion. After maximizing the use of raw and cooked veggies in my soups, I realized that there is no longer any need to stick to old ideas and traditions about what a soup or a dinner should be.

In the process, I became increasingly keen to eat seasonally, since that means eating what is naturally at its best and what is therefore naturally best for our bodies.

I also fell in love with preserving vegetables and food in a more natural way, like fermenting. That way we not only feed our bodies the nutrients we need, but we are introduced to a whole new batch of healthy bacteria that keep our guts super balanced.

I'm so looking forward to hearing what you think about this new adventure in bowl food. It's been an amazing journey for me, full of incredible discoveries. I've had fantastic encounters with people to whom I've asked many questions about what dinner means to them, what they crave, what they eat, what's comforting and why.

I believe a big part of our health comes from how we treat ourselves and the people around us. When we take time to eat slowly and mindfully, we are more aware of what we are eating and how our body reacts to it. Connecting with food is important, and connecting with people should be just as important. Enjoying meals with friends and family is so embedded in the Italian tradition that I always take it for granted, but more than ever I believe that a great supper can only be achieved by connecting with the people we love (no technology is allowed at the dinner table!).

Love, attention and time are the real superfoods.

SOUP BOWLS

SALMON, BROWN RICE, CARROT, PEAS & MISO

INGREDIENTS

50 g [2 oz] smoked salmon
50 g [2 oz] cooked brown rice
½ carrot, ribboned
handful of fresh peas
sprinkle of sesame seeds
handful of fresh chives

BROTH

1 tbsp miso paste
250 ml [1 cup] hot water

RAW

VEGETARIAN
ALTERNATIVE
*Add 50 g [2 oz]
feta cheese*

AVOCADO & CUCUMBER GAZPACHO

INGREDIENTS

*½ avocado, sliced
handful of spiralized cucumber
¼ red onion, thinly sliced
handful of fresh basil
1 tsp shelled hemp seeds
1 tsp poppy seeds*

BROTH

*blend together:
4 tomatoes
juice of 1 lime
sprinkle of chilli [red pepper] flakes
salt and black pepper*

RAW

VEGETARIAN
ALTERNATIVE

*Add 50 g [2 oz]
shaved pecorino cheese*

CAVOLO NERO, AVOCADO, CAULIFLOWER & SQUASH

INGREDIENTS

*handful of cavolo nero, stalks removed
handful of purple cauliflower florets
½ avocado, roughly chopped
handful of sprouted sunflower seeds
sprinkle of fresh thyme
olive oil, to drizzle*

CREAM

*blend together:
50 g [2 oz] raw squash
1 tsp ground ginger
200 ml [¾ cup] cold almond milk
handful of cashew nuts
salt and black pepper*

VEGETARIAN

OMNIVORE
ALTERNATIVE
*Add 50 g [2 oz] fried
smoked bacon
or pancetta*

BLUE CHEESE, ONION, RADISH
& ARTICHOKE CREAM

INGREDIENTS

*50 g [2 oz] blue cheese, chopped
handful of fresh basil
handful of pine nuts
½ roasted red onion
handful of radishes, sliced*

BROTH

*blend together:
1 roasted artichoke
125 ml [½ cup] single [light] cream
125 ml [½ cup] hot vegetable broth
salt and black pepper*

TUNA, BEETROOT, BROCCOLI, EDAMAME & FISH STOCK

INGREDIENTS

40 g [1½ oz] tuna sashimi
¼ beetroot [beet], spiralized
handful of long-stem broccoli, steamed
handful of edamame, steamed
1 tsp sesame seeds, toasted

BROTH

250 ml [1 cup] hot fish stock

VEGAN

VEGETARIAN ALTERNATIVE

Add a soft-boiled egg or even 50 g [2 oz] feta cheese

RED PEPPER, SWEET POTATO, CAVOLO NERO & TRUFFLE

INGREDIENTS

1 roasted red [bell] pepper
50 g [2 oz] cavolo nero, chopped
handful of fresh parsley
handful of cooked butter beans
½ sweet potato, roasted
sprinkle of sunflower seeds, toasted

BROTH

250 ml [1 cup] hot vegetable broth
2 fresh sage leaves
drizzle of truffle oil
salt and black pepper

BEEF, PEAS, WATERCRESS, CARROT & BEEF BROTH

INGREDIENTS

*50 g [2 oz] beef, thinly sliced and boiled for
  20 minutes in the stock*
handful of watercress
1 small carrot, ribboned
handful of fresh peas
handful of pumpkin seeds, toasted

BROTH

300 ml [1¼ cups] hot beef stock
1 tsp miso paste
3 spring onions [scallions], sliced
salt and black pepper

FETA, CUCUMBER, MILLET, CARROT & PEPPER CREAM

INGREDIENTS

50 g [2 oz] feta cheese
50 g [2 oz] cooked millet
100 g [3½ oz] ribboned cucumber
handful of pickled ribboned carrots
handful of fresh parsley

CREAM

blend together:
2 roasted red [bell] peppers
200 ml [¾ cup] warm single [light] cream
drizzle of extra virgin olive oil
salt and black pepper

PESCATARIAN

VEGETARIAN
ALTERNATIVE
*Replace the fish with
a soft-boiled egg*

SALMON, BUCKWHEAT, CARROT, WATERCRESS & MISO

INGREDIENTS

*50 g [2 oz] salmon sashimi
50 g [2 oz] cooked buckwheat
¼ purple carrot, ribboned
handful of watercress
3 spring onions [scallions], sliced
sprinkle of steamed seaweed
sprinkle of black sesame seeds*

BROTH

*200 ml [¾ cup] hot water
1 tbsp miso paste*

BEETROOT, CARROT, CASHEW & SAUERKRAUT

INGREDIENTS

*100 g [3½ oz] spiralized beetroot [beet]
1 small carrot, grated
1 tbsp sauerkraut
1 spring onion [scallion], thinly sliced
sprinkle of caraway seeds*

CREAM

*blend together:
handful of cashew nuts
1 tbsp lemon juice
200 ml [¾ cup] cold water*

VEGAN

VEGETARIAN ALTERNATIVE

Replace the coconut milk with single [light] cream or plain yogurt

AUBERGINE, ONION, TURMERIC & RED LENTIL BROTH

INGREDIENTS

¼ roasted aubergine [eggplant]
½ red onion, roasted
1 tbsp Turmeric & Mustard Sauerkraut
  (page 42)
handful of fresh coriander [cilantro]
1 spring onion [scallion], sliced

CREAM

blend together:
250ml [1 cup] coconut milk
150 g [1 cup] cooked red split lentils
1 tbsp ground turmeric
1 tsp sesame seeds
salt and black pepper

CHICKEN, RED RICE, PEPPER & COCONUT MILK

INGREDIENTS

*100 g [3½ oz] cooked red rice
1 roasted red [bell] pepper
handful of brown mushrooms, roasted
50 g [2 oz] roasted chicken
handful of fresh coriander [cilantro]*

CREAM

*250 ml [1 cup] warm coconut milk
sprinkle of chilli [red pepper] flakes
salt and black pepper*

VEGETARIAN

VEGAN ALTERNATIVE

*Replace the cheese
with cooked chickpeas*

BLUE CHEESE, RADICCHIO, SWEET POTATO & BROTH

INGREDIENTS

handful of chopped cavolo nero
handful of spiralized sweet potato, stir-fried
50 g [2 oz] crumbled blue cheese
handful of fresh tarragon
handful of radicchio, roasted

BROTH

250 ml [1 cup] hot vegetable broth
salt and black pepper

PRAWNS, BROWN RICE, BROCCOLI & FISH BROTH

INGREDIENTS

*handful of cooked Atlantic prawns [shrimp]
50 g [2 oz] cooked brown rice
handful of long-stem broccoli, steamed
handful of fresh chives
sprinkle of chia seeds*

BROTH

*boil together for 15 minutes:
handful of rainbow chard
250 ml [1 cup] fish stock
1 tbsp fish sauce or anchovy paste*

SQUID, NOODLES, KALE, RED ONION & WHITE MISO CREAM

INGREDIENTS

1 small squid, sliced and griddled
100 g [3½ oz] cooked rice noodles
handful of purple kale, lightly steamed
1 small red onion, roasted
sprinkle of red amaranth cress

CREAM

250 ml [1 cup] warm single [light] cream
1 tsp lemon juice
1 tbsp white miso paste
sprinkle of chilli [red pepper] flakes
salt and black pepper

VEGAN

VEGETARIAN ALTERNATIVE

Add 50 g [2 oz] goats' cheese or smoked sheep cheese

KALE, SUN-DRIED TOMATOES, MUSHROOMS & TRUFFLE

INGREDIENTS

4 sun-dried tomatoes, soaked overnight
handful of purple kale, chopped
2 tbsp cooked butter beans
1 flat mushroom, roasted with 1 tbsp tamari
handful of fresh parsley
sprinkle of sesame seeds

BROTH

250 ml [1 cup] hot vegetable broth
2 tbsp beetroot [beet] juice
1 tsp truffle oil
salt and black pepper

RAW

VEGETARIAN ALTERNATIVE

Add 50 g [2 oz] shaved pecorino cheese

COURGETTI, BROCCOLI, SUN-DRIED TOMATOES & BASIL

INGREDIENTS

handful of whole almonds
1 courgette [zucchini], spiralized
handful of long-stem broccoli, blanched
6 sun-dried tomatoes, soaked overnight
handful of fresh basil

BROTH

blend together:
1 tbsp extra virgin olive oil
250 ml [1 cup] cold almond milk
handful of cashew nuts
big handful of fresh basil
salt and black pepper

RAW

VEGETARIAN
ALTERNATIVE
*Add 50 g [2 oz]
goats' cheese*

RADICCHIO, RADISH, PISTACHIO & CELERIAC CREAM

INGREDIENTS

*handful of shredded radicchio
3 radishes, thinly sliced
handful of pistachios
handful of fresh parsley*

CREAM

*blend together:
50 g [2 oz] celeriac, chopped
handful of cashew nuts
125 ml [½ cup] cold water
1 tbsp extra virgin olive oil
salt and black pepper*

MACKEREL, SWEET POTATO & CAVOLO NERO

INGREDIENTS

50 g [2 oz] smoked mackerel
handful of cavolo nero, steamed
½ small red onion, roasted
¼ sweet potato, spiralized and roasted
handful of fresh dill

CREAM

1 tbsp smoked paprika
200 ml [¾ cup] warm single [light]
  cream
1 tsp olive oil
salt and black pepper

EGG, PEA, PARSNIP, COCONUT & TURMERIC

INGREDIENTS

1 hard-boiled egg
¼ small parsnip, ribboned
¼ red onion, thinly sliced
50 g [2 oz] steamed fresh peas
sprinkle of radish sprouts
sprinkle of black sesame seeds

BROTH

1 tbsp ground turmeric
1 tbsp cayenne pepper
250 ml [1 cup] warm coconut milk
250 ml [1 cup] hot water
salt and black pepper

OMNIVORE

VEGAN
ALTERNATIVE
Replace the chicken with 50 g [2 oz] cooked lentils, and the chicken stock with veg stock

SPELT TAGLIATELLE, ROASTED CHICKEN, CHARD & MISO

INGREDIENTS

50 g [2 oz] cooked spelt tagliatelle
50 g [2 oz] chicken breast, roasted
100 g [3½ oz] Jerusalem artichokes, roasted
handful of rainbow chard, boiled with the stock for a few minutes
handful of fresh parsley

BROTH

200 ml [¾ cup] hot chicken stock
1 tsp miso paste
salt and black pepper

RICOTTA, MUSHROOM, KALE & TRUFFLE CREAM

INGREDIENTS

1 portobello mushroom, sliced and fried
handful of purple kale, steamed then fried
50 g [2 oz] cooked spaghetti
1 tbsp ricotta
handful of fresh chives
handful of pumpkin seeds, toasted

CREAM

heat up together:
200 ml [¾ cup] single [light] cream
sprinkle of chilli [red pepper] flakes
drizzle of balsamic glaze
drizzle of truffle oil
salt and black pepper

VEGAN

OMINVORE ALTERNATIVE

Add 50 g [2 oz] roasted chicken

MUSHROOM, EDAMAME, CORN, COCONUT CREAM & BROTH

INGREDIENTS

1 pak choi, finely chopped
handful of steamed edamame beans
2 portobello mushrooms, sliced and roasted
handful of fresh chives
handful of steamed baby corn
sprinkle of black sesame seeds

BROTH

250 ml [1 cup] hot vegetable stock
drizzle of olive oil
1 tbsp coconut cream
salt and black pepper

RAW

VEGETARIAN
ALTERNATIVE
Add a soft-boiled egg

CARROT, GOJI, SAUERKRAUT, & AVOCADO & PEA CREAM

INGREDIENTS

handful of ribboned purple carrot
2 tbsp Turmeric & Mustard Sauerkraut
  (page 42)
sprinkle of fresh dill
handful of goji berries, soaked for 10 minutes
sprinkle of shelled hemp seeds

CREAM

blend together:
80 g [½ cup] fresh peas
1 avocado
salt and black pepper

PRAWNS, SEAWEED, RED ONIONS & MILLET

INGREDIENTS

handful of cooked Atlantic prawns [shrimp]
cooked 100 g [3½ oz] millet or amaranth
1 roasted small red onion
handful of pumpkin seeds, toasted
1 spring onion [scallion], sliced
sprinkle of red amaranth

BROTH

250 ml [1 cup] hot fish stock
1 tbsp miso paste
handful of seaweed "spaghetti"
* cooked like pasta in the broth*

RAW

VEGETARIAN
ALTERNATIVE
Add a soft-boiled egg

KALE, AVOCADO, TOMATOES & LEMON CARROT SMOOTHIE

INGREDIENTS

handful of kale, massaged with lemon juice
½ avocado
handful of cherry tomatoes, halved
handful of radish sprouts
sprinkle of black sesame seeds

CREAM

blend together:
125 ml [½ cup] carrot juice
½ avocado
1 tbsp lemon juice
1 yellow carrot
salt and black pepper

PESCATARIAN

VEGETARIAN ALTERNATIVE

Replace the cod with goats' cheese

COD, NOODLES, SWEET POTATO, CHARD & PEA CREAM

INGREDIENTS

50 g [2 oz] poached cod
50 g [2 oz] cooked black rice noodles
handful of ribboned sweet potato, stir-fried
handful of ribboned rainbow chard, stir-fried
handful of fresh tarragon
sprinkle of chia seeds

CREAM

blend together:
250 ml [1 cup] warm single [light] cream
handful of fresh peas
1 tsp extra virgin olive oil
salt and black pepper

HALLOUMI, BARLEY, SQUASH
& BEETROOT CREAM

INGREDIENTS

50 g [2 oz] halloumi, sliced and fried
50 g [2 oz] cooked pearl barley
50 g [2 oz] squash, roasted
handful of ribboned purple carrot
handful of fresh coriander [cilantro]

CREAM

blend and warm up together:
50 ml [3½ tbsp] beetroot [beet] juice
150 ml [⅔ cup] single [light] cream
50 g [2 oz] red onion, roasted
salt and black pepper

ANCHOVIES, BEETROOT, CARROT & BUCKWHEAT

INGREDIENTS

4 anchovies
100 g [3½ oz] cooked buckwheat
¼ carrot, ribboned
½ raw candy beetroot, spiralized
handful of fresh parsley

BROTH

blend together:
250 ml [1 cup] warm rice cream
1 tbsp grated fresh ginger
zest and juice of ½ lemon
salt and black pepper

CHICKEN, RICE, AUBERGINE, RED PEPPER & COCONUT

INGREDIENTS

50 g [2 oz] fried chicken pieces
50 g [2 oz] cooked white rice
70 g [2½ oz] diced aubergine [eggplant], roasted
1 red [bell] pepper, roasted
handful of fresh coriander [cilantro]

CREAM

200 ml [¾ cup] warm coconut milk
1 tbsp ground turmeric
1 tbsp grated fresh ginger
juice of 1 lemon
salt and black pepper

PESCATARIAN

VEGAN
ALTERNATIVE

*Replace the salmon
with roasted tofu*

SALMON, BABY KALE, PEAS, TURMERIC & COCONUT

INGREDIENTS

*50 g [2 oz] honey-roasted salmon
handful of baby kale
handful of fresh peas
1 roasted red [bell] pepper
handful of fresh chives*

BROTH

*250 ml [1 cup] warm coconut milk
1 tsp ground ginger
1 tsp ground turmeric
juice of ½ lemon
salt and black pepper*

RAW

VEGAN ALTERNATIVE

Add 50 g [2 oz] cooked beans of your choice

CAULIFLOWER, AVOCADO, DILL, RADISH & SPINACH

INGREDIENTS

¼ cauliflower, blended to "rice"
1 avocado, diced
4 radishes, thinly sliced
handful of fresh dill
1 tsp chia seeds

BROTH

blend together:
200 ml [¾ cup] cold water
handful of spinach
handful of fresh dill
1 tbsp olive oil
salt and black pepper

VEGETARIAN

VEGAN ALTERNATIVE

Replace the egg with 50 g [2 oz] smoked or fried tofu

EGG, PARSNIP, CORIANDER, GINGER & COCONUT

INGREDIENTS

1 soft-boiled egg
¼ red onion, thinly sliced
¼ parsnip, ribboned
handful of long-stem broccoli, steamed
sprinkle of fresh coriander [cilantro]
sprinkle of sesame seeds

BROTH

1 tbsp grated fresh ginger
125 ml [½ cup] warm coconut milk
125 ml [½ cup] hot water
salt and black pepper

OMNIVORE

VEGETARIAN
ALTERNATIVE
*Replace the meatballs
with 50 g [2 oz]
scamorza cheese*

MEATBALLS, ONION, CHARD, WILD RICE & YOGURT

INGREDIENTS

*1 roasted onion, sliced
handful of steamed baby rainbow chard
3 meatballs, roasted
100 g [3½ oz] cooked wild rice
sprinkle of fresh thyme*

CREAM

*200 ml [¾ cup] warm plain yogurt
drizzle of olive oil
salt and black pepper*

CARROT, BEETROOT, QUINOA & YOGURT

INGREDIENTS

1 carrot, ribboned
¼ raw beetroot [beet], shaved into "petals" with a vegetable peeler
100 g [3½ oz] cooked red quinoa
handful of cashews, toasted
sprinkle of fresh lemon thyme

BROTH

250 g [1 cup] plain yogurt
squeeze of lemon juice
salt and black pepper

RAW

VEGAN
ALTERNATIVE
*Add a handful of
steamed green peas*

COURGETTE, PICKLED RADISH
& TOMATO SMOOTHIE

INGREDIENTS

*½ courgette [zucchini], spiralized
handful of cherry tomatoes, halved
handful of pickled radish
handful of fresh dill
1 tbsp black sesame seeds*

BROTH

*blend together:
1 tbsp extra virgin olive oil
450 g [3 cups] cherry tomatoes
¼ tsp cayenne pepper
salt and black pepper*

VEGAN

PESCATARIAN
ALTERNATIVE
*Add 50 g [2 oz]
cooked prawns*

BABY CORN, BROCCOLI, PEAS, GINGER & COCONUT

INGREDIENTS

*handful of fresh peas
handful of baby corn, steamed
handful of long-stem broccoli, steamed
handful of fresh coriander [cilantro]
1 spring onion [scallion], sliced
sprinkle of chilli [red pepper] flakes*

CREAM

*blend together:
250 ml [1 cup] warm coconut milk
handful of fresh peas
1 tsp ground ginger
salt and black pepper*

SAUSAGE, RICE, RADISH, CUCUMBER & KIMCHI

INGREDIENTS

handful of spiralized cucumber
handful of radishes, thinly sliced
50 g [2 oz] cooked jasmine rice
50 g [2 oz] pork sausage, roasted
small bunch of fresh chives
sprinkle of poppy seeds

BROTH

200 ml [¾ cup] hot vegetable stock
1 tsp miso paste
1 tbsp kimchi
salt and black pepper

RAW

PESCATARIAN
ALTERNATIVE
*Add 50 g [2 oz]
roasted wild salmon*

KALE, CARROT, RED PEPPER, CASHEW & COCONUT

INGREDIENTS

handful of cashew nuts
handful of purple kale, chopped
½ carrot, ribboned
¼ red [bell] pepper, thinly sliced
handful of fresh coriander [cilantro]
sprinkle of chia seeds

BROTH

320 ml [1½ cups] cold coconut milk
1 tsp ground ginger
salt and black pepper

VEGETARIAN ALTERNATIVE

Replace the meatballs with a soft-boiled egg

MEATBALLS, BUCKWHEAT, BEETROOT & SOUR CREAM

INGREDIENTS

3 meatballs, roasted
1 roasted red onion, sliced
100 g [3½ oz] cooked buckwheat
handful of fresh dill
1 tbsp sauerkraut flavoured with caraway

CREAM

blend together:
1 roasted beetroot [beet], grated
1 tsp chilli powder
200 ml [¾ cup] hot vegetable broth
2 tbsp sour cream
salt and black pepper

PESCATARIAN

VEGETARIAN
ALTERNATIVE
*Replace the cod with
50 g [2 oz] scamorza
cheese*

COD, KALE, RED ONION, BASIL & TOMATO SOUP

INGREDIENTS

*1 cod fillet, poached
handful of purple kale, massaged with lemon
½ red onion, thinly sliced
handful of fresh basil
handful of toasted pine nuts*

BROTH

*250 ml [1 cup] warm tomato sauce
drizzle of olive oil
salt and black pepper*

OMNIVORE

VEGAN ALTERNATIVE
Replace the chorizo with 2 tbsp cooked black beans, and the single cream with soya cream

CHORIZO, CELERIAC, KALE & CAULIFLOWER

INGREDIENTS

50 g [2 oz] chorizo, roasted
100 g [3½ oz] diced celeriac, roasted
100 g [3½ oz] cauliflower florets, roasted
handful of purple kale, steamed
handful of fresh parsley

CREAM

200 ml [¾ cup] warm single [light] cream
1 tsp lemon juice
salt and black pepper

VEGAN

PESCATARIAN ALTERNATIVE

Add a handful of cooked prawns

BROCCOLI, MUSHROOMS, TURMERIC & COCONUT

INGREDIENTS

handful of purple sprouting broccoli, steamed
handful of brown mushrooms, roasted
50 g [2 oz] steamed fresh peas
handful of red amaranth
handful of purple kale, massaged with a
  squeeze of lemon juice

BROTH

1 tbsp ground turmeric
1 tbsp grated fresh ginger
250 ml [1 cup] warm coconut milk
250 ml [1 cup] hot water
sprinkle of chilli [red pepper] flakes
salt and black pepper

VEGAN

VEGETARIAN ALTERNATIVE

Add 50 g [2 oz] goats' cheese or a soft-boiled egg

KALE, MUSHROOM, BUTTER BEANS & SAGE

INGREDIENTS

handful of raw kale, massaged in warm water
¼ red onion, sliced
1 flat white mushroom, roasted with 1 tbsp tamari soy sauce
2 tbsp cooked butter beans

BROTH

the liquid from the mushroom
250 ml [1 cup] hot vegetable broth
2 sage leaves
salt and black pepper

EGG, WILD RICE, ASPARAGUS, ONION & SAFFRON CREAM

INGREDIENTS

*a soft-boiled egg
100 g [3½ oz] cooked wild rice
4 asparagus spears, roasted
1 onion, roasted and sliced
handful of fresh dill*

CREAM

*pinch of saffron threads
200 ml [¾ cup] warm single [light]
  cream
drizzle of olive oil
salt and black pepper*

VEGAN

VEGETARIAN
ALTERNATIVE
*Add a poached or
soft-boiled egg*

QUINOA, TOMATO, CORN, BLACK PEAS & PAPRIKA

INGREDIENTS

*50 g [2 oz] cooked black/carlin peas
handful of cherry tomatoes, roasted
handful of fresh corn kernels
2 tbsp cooked red quinoa
handful of fresh parsley or coriander
 [cilantro]*

BROTH

*200 ml [¾ cup] hot vegetable stock
pinch of chilli [red pepper] flakes
pinch of smoked paprika
salt and black pepper*

PESCATARIAN

VEGAN
ALTERNATIVE

*Replace the mackerel
with more peas*

MACKEREL, NOODLES, PAK CHOI & PAPRIKA CREAM

INGREDIENTS

*50 g [2 oz] smoked mackerel
50 g [2 oz] cooked black rice noodles
handful of steamed or fresh peas
handful of pak choi, lightly steamed
handful of fresh chives
sprinkle of sesame seeds, toasted*

CREAM

*200 ml [¾ cup] warm coconut milk
1 tsp smoked paprika
salt and black pepper*

CUCUMBER, AVOCADO, MINT, POMEGRANATE & GINGER

INGREDIENTS

*handful of sunflower seeds
handful of spiralized cucumber
½ avocado, sliced
handful of pomegranate seeds
handful of fresh mint
pinch of poppy seeds*

CREAM

*200 ml [¾ cup] cold almond milk
1 tbsp grated fresh ginger
pinch of salt
olive oil, to drizzle*

OMNIVORE

VEGAN ALTERNATIVE
Replace the chicken with fried tofu, and the yogurt with oat or rice cream

CHICKEN, CUCUMBER, AVOCADO & CORN CREAM

INGREDIENTS

50 g [2 oz] fried chicken breast pieces
handful of spiralized cucumber
½ avocado, diced
6 sun-dried tomatoes, soaked overnight
handful of fresh coriander [cilantro]
70 g [2½ oz] cooked black beans

CREAM

blend together, then heat up:
200 ml [¾ cup] plain yogurt
handful of fresh corn kernels
pinch of chilli [red pepper] flakes
1 tsp extra virgin olive oil
salt and black pepper

PRAWNS, TOMATOES, COURGETTE & FISH STOCK

INGREDIENTS

handful of cooked Atlantic prawns [shrimp]
100 g [3½ oz] julienned courgette [zucchini]
handful of chopped spring onions [scallions]
handful of fresh baby parsley
sprinkle of black sesame seeds

BROTH

boil together:
250 ml [1 cup] fish stock
handful of cherry tomatoes
1 tsp chilli [red pepper] flakes
salt and black pepper

VEGETARIAN

VEGAN
ALTERNATIVE
*Replace the goats'
cheese with 2 tbsp cooked
black lentils, and the
cream with oat
cream*

PEAS, COURGETTE, SWEET POTATO & GOATS' CHEESE

INGREDIENTS

*handful of spiralized courgette [zucchini]
½ sweet potato, spiralized and roasted
handful of steamed fresh peas
50 g [2 oz] goats' cheese
handful of fresh chives*

CREAM

*blend together:
200 ml [¾ cup] warm single [light]
  cream
1 tsp olive oil
handful of fresh peas
salt and black pepper*

VEGAN ALTERNATIVE

Replace the chicken with fried tofu, and the single cream with oat or rice cream

CHICKEN, RED ONION, CARROT & MUSTARD SPROUTS

INGREDIENTS

50 g [2 oz] roasted chicken
½ red onion, thinly sliced
1 small carrot, ribboned
handful of mustard sprouts

BROTH

250 ml [1 cup] hot chicken or vegetable broth
2 tbsp single [light] cream
squeeze of lemon juice

VEGAN

OMNIVORE ALTERNATIVE
Add 50 g [2 oz] roast beef or pork

QUINOA, YELLOW PEAS, MUSHROOMS & MISO

INGREDIENTS

50 g [2 oz] cooked yellow split peas
50 g [2 oz] cooked red quinoa
handful of shiitake mushrooms, fried
handful of baby spinach
handful of fresh chives
sprinkle of sesame seeds, toasted

BROTH

boil together for 10 minutes:
1 tbsp miso paste
200 ml [¾ cup] water or vegetable
  stock
handful of dried dulse seaweed
salt and black pepper

RICOTTA, COURGETTE, SPINACH & ASPARAGUS

INGREDIENTS

1 tbsp fresh ricotta cheese
½ courgette [zucchini], spiralized
4 asparagus tips, roasted
6 sun-dried tomatoes, soaked overnight
handful of pumpkin seeds, toasted
sprinkle of red amaranth

BROTH

blend together:
150 ml [⅔ cup] ricotta
handful of baby spinach
the bottoms of the 4 asparagus

VEGETARIAN

OMNIVORE
ALTERNATIVE

*Replace the egg with
50 g [2 oz] salt beef*

EGG, BROCCOLI, PEAS, RICE NOODLES & MISO

INGREDIENTS

1 soft-boiled egg
½ small carrot, julienned
handful of long-stem broccoli, steamed
handful of fresh peas
handful of cooked black rice noodles
1 tbsp crispy fried onions

BROTH

1 tbsp miso paste
250 ml [1 cup] hot vegetable broth
sprinkle of chilli [red pepper] flakes

ASPARAGUS, RADICCHIO, BLACK BEANS & PARSNIP CREAM

INGREDIENTS

handful of long-stem broccoli, steamed
70 g [½ cup] cooked black beans
¼ radicchio, roasted
6 asparagus spears, roasted
handful of fresh parsley

CREAM

blend together:
½ parsnip, roasted
250 ml [1 cup] warm oat cream
drizzle of extra virgin olive oil
salt and black pepper

VEGAN

PESCATARIAN ALTERNATIVE
Add 50 g [2 oz] roasted wild salmon

CAVOLO NERO, JERUSALEM ARTICHOKES & TRUFFLE

INGREDIENTS

*50 g [2 oz] cooked buckwheat noodles
handful of cavolo nero, lightly steamed
100 g [3½ oz] Jerusalem artichokes,
  sliced and roasted
2 tbsp cooked red kidney beans
sprinkle of fresh thyme and sesame seeds*

BROTH

*boil together for 15 minutes:
200 ml [¾ cup] vegetable broth
handful of dried porcini mushrooms
  (strain these out after cooking)
salt and black pepper
drizzle of truffle oil, to serve*

RAW

PESCATARIAN ALTERNATIVE

Add 50 g [2 oz] cooked prawns

PEAS, BROCCOLI, SAUERKRAUT & TURMERIC CREAM

INGREDIENTS

handful of broccoli florets
handful of fresh chives
handful of fresh peas and shredded spinach
handful of Turmeric & Mustard
  Sauerkraut (page 42)
sprinkle of chia seeds

CREAM

blend together:
handful of cashew nuts
250 ml [1 cup] cold coconut milk
1 tbsp ground turmeric
salt and black pepper

OMNIVORE
ALTERNATIVE

*Add 50 g [2 oz]
salt beef*

SPINACH, ASPARAGUS, BEETROOT & PEPPER

INGREDIENTS

*handful of fresh spinach, shredded
2 asparagus spears, ribboned
¼ raw beetroot [beet], shaved into "petals"
  with a vegetable peeler
handful of fresh coriander [cilantro]
pinch of chia seeds*

CREAM

*blend together:
½ red [bell] pepper
1 tbsp tahini
pinch of chilli [red pepper] flakes
200 ml [¾ cup] cold water*

VEGAN

VEGETARIAN ALTERNATIVE
Add 50 g [2 oz] blue cheese

SWEET POTATO, CAULIFLOWER, BLACK LENTILS & MISO

INGREDIENTS

200 g [1 cup] cooked black lentils
½ large sweet potato, roasted
handful of cauliflower florets, roasted
2 tbsp cooked quinoa
sprinkle of fresh thyme
sprinkle of sesame seeds, toasted

BROTH

250ml [1 cup] hot vegetable stock
1 tbsp miso paste
salt and black pepper

VEGETARIAN

PESCATARIAN ALTERNATIVE

Replace the mozzarella with 50 g [2 oz] poached cod

MOZZARELLA, BROCCOLI, BASIL, OLIVES & TOMATO CREAM

INGREDIENTS

handful of mini mozzarella balls
handful of long-stem broccoli, steamed
handful of fresh basil
handful of black olives
handful of pine nuts

CREAM

blend together:
225 g [1½ cups] cherry tomatoes
1 tbsp extra virgin olive oil
salt and black pepper

BACON, BROCCOLI, RED PEPPER & TAGLIATELLE

INGREDIENTS

1 roasted red [bell] pepper, sliced
handful of steamed long-stem broccoli
40 g [1½ oz] cooked spelt tagliatelle
2 slices of bacon, grilled [broiled]
sprinkle of fresh thyme
sprinkle of toasted sesame seeds

BROTH

250 ml [1 cup] warm beef broth
drizzle of olive oil
salt and black pepper

VEGAN

OMNIVORE ALTERNATIVE

Add 50 g [2 oz] roasted chicken

MUSHROOM, CARROT, BEANS, BUCKWHEAT & TRUFFLE

INGREDIENTS

170 g [1 cup] cooked buckwheat
50 g [2 oz] mushrooms, roasted with tamari
handful of ribboned white heritage carrot
2 tbsp cooked butter beans
handful of pumpkin seeds, toasted
1 tbsp pickled sliced radish

BROTH

250ml [1 cup] hot vegetable broth
drizzle of truffle oil
sprinkle of red amaranth cress

OMNIVORE

PESCATARIAN
ALTERNATIVE
Replace the beef with
50 g [2 oz] cooked
Atlantic prawns

BEEF, COURGETTE, RED CABBAGE & COCONUT

INGREDIENTS

50 g [2 oz] salt beef
½ courgette [zucchini], spiralized
3 spring onions [scallions] chopped
1 tbsp Spicy Red Sauerkraut (page 42)
handful of fresh coriander [cilantro]
handful of pumpkin seeds, toasted

CREAM

200 ml [¾ cup] warm coconut milk
1 tsp ground ginger
sprinkle of chilli [red pepper] flakes
salt and black pepper

CHORIZO, BROWN RICE, MUSHROOMS & BROTH

INGREDIENTS

100 g [3½ oz] cooked brown rice
100 g [3½ oz] Jerusalem artichokes, roasted
50 g [2 oz] chorizo, roasted
100 g [3½ oz] oyster mushrooms, roasted
sprinkle of sesame seeds
handful of fresh parsley

BROTH

250 ml [1 cup] hot vegetable stock
1 tsp miso paste

VEGAN

PESCATARIAN ALTERNATIVE

Add 50 g [2 oz] cooked prawns

SQUASH, CARROT, LENTILS, & COCONUT & TURMERIC CREAM

INGREDIENTS

1 purple carrot, ribboned and roasted
handful of diced squash, roasted
100 g [3½ oz] cooked buckwheat
handful of garlic chives
spinkle of sesame seeds
1 tbsp Spicy Red Sauerkraut (page 42)
50 g [2 oz] cooked beluga lentils

CREAM

250 ml [1 cup] warm coconut milk
1 tsp ground ginger
1 tsp ground turmeric
juice of ½ lemon
salt and black pepper

NOURISHING BOWLS

VEGAN

VEGETARIAN
ALTERNATIVE
Add 50 g [2 oz]
goats' cheese

BUCKWHEAT, PEAS, AVOCADO, MUSHROOMS & MUSTARD

INGREDIENTS

100 g [3½ oz] cooked buckwheat
½ avocado, sliced
2 roasted portobello mushrooms, sliced
handful of pumpkin seeds, toasted
handful of blanched fresh peas
sprinkle of red amaranth cress

DRESSING

1 tbsp mustard
1 tsp cider vinegar
1 tbsp extra virgin olive oil
1 tsp maple syrup
salt and black pepper

VEGETARIAN

VEGAN
ALTERNATIVE
Replace the
mozzarella with
chickpeas and the
pecorino with
tahini

KALE, MOZZARELLA, SQUASH, CAULIFLOWER & PARSLEY PESTO

INGREDIENTS

handful of mozzarella balls
handful of purple kale, steamed
100 g [3½ oz] squash, roasted
100 g [3½ oz] cauliflower florets, roasted
handful of fresh parsley
handful of toasted pine nuts

PESTO

blend together:
handful of parsley
handful of pine nuts
1 tbsp shaved pecorino cheese
2 tbsp extra virgin olive oil
salt and black pepper

VEGAN

PESCATARIAN
ALTERNATIVE
*Add 50 g [2 oz]
cooked sustainably-
sourced tuna*

CUCUMBER, MIZUNA, PEAS, TAMARI & SEAWEED

INGREDIENTS

*handful of blanched fresh peas
handful of spiralized cucumber
handful of mizuna or rocket [arugula] leaves
handful of fresh corn kernels
sprinkle of red amaranth cress*

SAUCE

*1 tsp tamari soy sauce
1 tbsp extra virgin olive oil
sprinkle of nori seaweed
1 tsp tahini
salt and black pepper*

FETA, CARROT, QUINOA & MUSTARD

INGREDIENTS

½ small heritage carrot, ribboned
½ roasted red [bell] pepper, chopped
50 g [2 oz] cooked black/carlin peas
sprinkle of lemon thyme
50 g [½ cup] crumbled feta cheese
100 g [3½ oz] cooked quinoa

DRESSING

1 tbsp extra virgin olive oil
1 tsp tahini
1 tsp lemon juice
1 tsp Dijon mustard
little squeeze of date or maple syrup
salt and black pepper

EGG, RICE, BROCCOLI, ONION, WASABI & GINGER SAUCE

INGREDIENTS

1 hard-boiled egg
100 g [3½ oz] cooked red camargue rice
handful of long-stem broccoli, steamed
½ small red onion, thinly sliced
handful of fresh tarragon
sprinkle of toasted sesame seeds

SAUCE

pinch of wasabi powder
pinch of ground ginger
1 tbsp mayonnaise
1 tbsp extra virgin olive oil
salt and black pepper

RAW

PESCATARIAN ALTERNATIVE
*Add 50 g [2 oz]
cooked Atlantic prawns*

CAULIFLOWER, GRAPEFRUIT, POMEGRANATE & DATES

INGREDIENTS

½ small cauliflower, blended to "rice"
½ grapefruit, chopped
handful of pomegranate seeds
1 tbsp pistachios
handful of dates
handful of fresh tarragon

DRESSING

1 tbsp extra virgin olive oil
1 tsp lemon juice
1 tsp tahini
salt and black pepper

PESCATARIAN

VEGETARIAN ALTERNATIVE

Replace the mackerel with a hard- or soft-boiled egg

MACKEREL, QUINOA, RADISH, TARRAGON & TARTARE SAUCE

INGREDIENTS

50 g [2 oz] smoked mackerel
100 g [3½ oz] cooked red quinoa
handful of radishes, thinly sliced
100 g [3½ oz] cucumber, spiralized
handful of fresh tarragon
sprinkle of poppy seeds

SAUCE

2 tbsp tartare sauce
1 tbsp extra virgin olive oil
drizzle of lemon juice
salt and black pepper

OMNIVORE

VEGAN
ALTERNATIVE
*Replace the chicken
with pan-fried tofu and
the cheese with oat or
rice cream*

CHICKEN, AUBERGINE, RICE, RADICCHIO & FRESH CHEESE

INGREDIENTS

50 g [2 oz] roasted chicken breast pieces
100 g [3½ oz] cooked brown rice
½ aubergine [eggplant], roasted
¼ radicchio, roasted
handful of pistachios
handful of fresh tarragon

DRESSING

1 tbsp cottage cheese or ricotta
1 tbsp extra virgin olive oil
sprinkle of chilli [red pepper] flakes
salt and black pepper

VEGAN

RAW
ALTERNATIVE

*Replace the black
peas with a handful
of cashew nuts*

MIZUNA, BLACK PEAS,
CELERIAC & GOJI BERRIES

INGREDIENTS

*30 g [1 oz] red streak mizuna
handful of spiralized celeriac [celery root]
1 tbsp pickled sliced radish
50 g [2 oz] cooked black/carlin peas
sprinkle of sesame seeds
fennel microgreens*

DRESSING

*1 tbsp extra virgin olive oil
1 tsp tahini
1 tsp cider vinegar
sprinkle of goji berries, soaked for
  10 minutes
salt and black pepper*

YOGURT, CUCUMBER, PEPPER, RED ONION & OLIVES

INGREDIENTS

100 g [3½ oz] cucumber, spiralized
½ roasted yellow [bell] pepper, chopped
1 roasted red onion, sliced
handful of fresh dill
handful of black olives
sprinkle of black sesame seeds

SAUCE

2 tbsp plain yogurt
1 tbsp extra virgin olive oil
salt and black pepper

VEGAN

OMNIVORE
ALTERNATIVE
*Add 50 g [2 oz]
roasted pork or ham*

RICE, BEANS, MUSHROOMS, CUCUMBER & GOJI BERRIES

INGREDIENTS

*100 g [3½ oz] cooked jasmine rice
50 g [2 oz] cooked black-eyed beans
handful of goji berries, soaked for 10 minutes
handful of oyster mushrooms, roasted
handful of spiralized cucumber
handful of baby coriander [cilantro]*

DRESSING

*1 tsp tamari soy sauce
1 tbsp extra virgin olive oil
sprinkle of sesame seeds
1 tsp seaweed sprinkle*

VEGETARIAN

VEGAN ALTERNATIVE
Replace the egg with more peas and squash

EGG, PEAS, SQUASH & BUCKWHEAT

INGREDIENTS

1 hard-boiled egg
¼ butternut squash, chopped and steamed
100 g [3½ oz] cooked buckwheat
handful of blanched fresh peas
¼ red onion, thinly sliced
sprinkle of fresh thyme

DRESSING

1 tbsp extra virgin olive oil
1 tsp tahini
1 tsp lemon juice
1 tsp English mustard
little squeeze of date or maple syrup
salt and black pepper

MOZZARELLA, TORTIGLIONI, TOMATO & RADICCHIO

INGREDIENTS

handful of mini mozzarella balls
*70 g [2½ oz] cooked wholewheat tortiglioni
  pasta*
handful of cherry tomatoes
¼ radicchio, fried
bunch of fresh chives

DRESSING

2 tbsp extra virgin olive oil
sprinkle of sesame seeds
salt and black pepper

RAW

PESCATARIAN
ALTERNATIVE
*Add 50 g [2 oz]
cooked Atlantic prawns*

CORN, ROCKET, PEPPER, GUACAMOLE & CORIANDER

INGREDIENTS

*1 spring onion [scallion], sliced
½ red [bell] pepper, thinly sliced
handful of coriander [cilantro]
140 g [1 cup] fresh corn, pulsed in a blender
handful of rocket [arugula]
sprinkle of sesame and chia seeds*

SAUCE

*blend together:
1 avocado
1 tsp lemon juice
1 tbsp extra virgin olive oil
salt and black pepper*

VEGETARIAN

VEGAN ALTERNATIVE
Replace the egg with more black/carlin peas

EGG, QUINOA, CARROT, BROCCOLI & NORI

INGREDIENTS

1 soft-boiled egg
100 g [3½ oz] cooked quinoa
½ purple carrot, ribboned
50 g [2 oz] cooked black/carlin peas
handful of purple sprouting broccoli, steamed
red amaranth cress

SAUCE

1 tsp tamari soy sauce
1 tbsp extra virgin olive oil
sprinkle of nori seaweed
1 tsp tahini
salt and black pepper

VEGAN

VEGETARIAN ALTERNATIVE

Add a soft-boiled egg

BUCKWHEAT, CAULIFLOWER, BEETROOT & TAHINI

INGREDIENTS

handful of blanched fresh peas
100 g [3½ oz] cooked buckwheat
handful of pickled purple cauliflower
¼ small beetroot [beet], spiralized
handful of pumpkin seeds, toasted
handful of fresh parsley

SAUCE

blend together:
1 tbsp extra virgin olive oil
1 tbsp tahini
1 tbsp ground turmeric
salt and black pepper

RAW

VEGAN ALTERNATIVE

Add 50 g [2 oz] cooked cannellini beans

COURGETTI, RED ONION, BASIL, HEMP & TOMATO SAUCE

INGREDIENTS

½ courgette [zucchini], ribboned
½ small red onion, sliced
handful of fresh basil
1 tbsp shelled hemp seeds
1 tbsp nutritional yeast flakes

SAUCE

blend together:
150 g [1 cup] cherry tomatoes
1 tbsp extra virgin olive oil
salt and black pepper

VEGETARIAN

VEGAN ALTERNATIVE

Replace the cheese with 50 g [2 oz] cooked quinoa or cashew cheese

GOATS' CHEESE, COURGETTI, PEAS & JERUSALEM ARTICHOKE

INGREDIENTS

50 g [2 oz] goats' cheese
½ courgette [zucchini], peeled and spiralized
100 g [3½ oz] Jerusalem artichokes, roasted
handful of blanched fresh peas
handful of fresh tarragon
handful of chopped walnuts

DRESSING

2 tbsp extra virgin olive oil
salt and black pepper

VEGETARIAN

VEGAN ALTERNATIVE

Replace the cheese with 50 g [2 oz] cooked chickpeas

SALTED RICOTTA, COUSCOUS, OLIVES, BROCCOLI & RED ONION

INGREDIENT

50 g [2 oz] salted ricotta cheese, flaked
100 g [3½ oz] cooked spelt couscous
handful of black olives
¼ red onion, thinly sliced
handful of purple sprouting broccoli, steamed
handful of fresh parsley

DRESSING

1 tbsp tahini
1 tbsp extra virgin olive oil
1 tsp lemon juice
sprinkle of black sesame seeds
salt and black pepper

HALLOUMI, RICE, ARTICHOKES, PEPPER & TARRAGON

INGREDIENTS

*50 g [2 oz] halloumi, fried and sliced
handful of fresh tarragon
140 g [4½ oz] red rice, cooked
1 roasted red [bell] pepper
handful of cooked artichoke hearts
1 tbsp cooked chickpeas*

DRESSING

*1 tbsp lemon juice
2 tbsp extra virgin olive oil
2 tbsp tahini
sprinkle of black sesame seeds
salt and black pepper*

VEGAN

VEGETARIAN
ALTERNATIVE
*Add 50 g [2 oz]
fried halloumi cheese*

COUSCOUS, RED ONION, PEPPER & PAPRIKA

INGREDIENTS

*2 tbsp hummus
100 g [3½ oz] cooked couscous
1 red onion, roasted and chopped
1 red [bell] pepper, roasted and chopped
handful of fresh parsley
sprinkle of black sesame seeds*

DRESSING

*1 tbsp smoked paprika
2 tbsp extra virgin olive oil
1 tbsp cider vinegar
1 tsp tahini
salt and black pepper*

RAW

VEGETARIAN
ALTERNATIVE

*Replace the saffron
cashew mayo with classic
mayonnaise*

RED CABBAGE, CARROT, PEAS, & SAFFRON CASHEW MAYO

INGREDIENTS

100g [3½ oz] red cabbage, shredded
1 small yellow carrot, ribboned
handful of green peas
sprinkle of sliced spring onions [scallions]
sprinkle of black sesame seeds
handful of fresh baby parsley

SAUCE

blend together:
handful of cashew nuts
1 tsp lemon juice
2 tbsp extra virgin olive
pinch of saffron threads
salt and black pepper

RAW

OMNIVORE
ALTERNATIVE

*Add 50 g [2 oz]
roasted chicken breast*

OATS, RADISHES, BEETROOT, TURMERIC & TAHINI SAUCE

INGREDIENTS

*100 g [3½ oz] oats soaked for 10 minutes in
almond milk and a pinch of salt*
1 small beetroot [beet], pared into "petals"
3 radishes, thinly sliced
handful of fresh tarragon
handful of baby rainbow chard, chopped

SAUCE

1 tbsp lemon juice
1 tsp ground turmeric
1 tbsp tahini
1 tbsp extra virgin olive oil
handful of pine nuts
salt and black pepper

VEGETARIAN ALTERNATIVE
Replace the mackerel with 50 g [2 oz] goats' cheese

MACKEREL, BEETROOT, MUNG BEANS, RED ONION & PARSLEY

INGREDIENTS

50 g [2 oz] smoked mackerel
1 beetroot [beet], spiralized and steamed
handful of cooked mung beans
½ small red onion, roasted and chopped
handful of fresh parsley

DRESSING

1 tbsp extra virgin olive oil
1 tsp lemon juice
salt and black pepper

OATS, MUSHROOMS, SPINACH, WALNUTS & TRUFFLE OIL

INGREDIENTS

*100 g [3½ oz] oats soaked for 10 minutes in
  almond milk and a pinch of salt
handful of brown mushrooms, marinated in
  olive oil and a pinch of salt
handful of baby spinach
bunch of fresh chives*

DRESSING

*1 tbsp extra virgin olive oil
drizzle of truffle-infused olive oil
handful of walnuts*

MEATBALLS, RICE, AVOCADO, TOMATOES & PAPRIKA SAUCE

INGREDIENTS

3 beef meatballs, roasted
handful of coriander [cilantro]
100 g [3½ oz] cooked jasmine rice
1 spring onion [scallion], thinly sliced
handful of cherry tomatoes, halved
½ avocado, chopped

SAUCE

1 tbsp extra virgin olive oil
1 tbsp tahini
1 tsp lemon juice
1 tsp smoked paprika
sprinkle of chilli [red pepper] flakes
salt and black pepper

143

PESCATARIAN

VEGETARIAN ALTERNATIVE
Replace the squid with 50 g [2 oz] goats' cheese

SQUID, BLACK QUINOA, TOMATOES & PARSLEY

INGREDIENTS

1 small squid, cleaned, sliced and grilled
100 g [3½ oz] cooked black quinoa
handful of cherry tomatoes, halved
½ red onion, thinly sliced
handful of fresh baby parsley
sprinkle of sesame seeds

SAUCE

handful of Parsley Pesto (page 119)
1 tbsp extra virgin olive oil
sprinkle of chilli [red pepper] flakes
salt and black pepper

KALE, AVOCADO, BEETROOT, APPLE & APRICOTS

INGREDIENTS

*50 g [2 oz] kale, massaged with lemon juice
1 apple, chopped and mixed with lemon juice
handful of dried apricots
handful of walnuts
handful of fresh tarragon*

SAUCE

*blend together:
½ beetroot [beet], grated
½ avocado
1 tsp lemon juice
salt and black pepper*

PESCATARIAN

VEGETARIAN ALTERNATIVE
Replace the anchovies
with 50 g [2 oz]
halloumi, fried

ANCHOVIES, BROCCOLI, PEAS, COUSCOUS & LEMON

INGREDIENTS

4 anchovies
100 g [3½ oz] cooked couscous
handful of long-stem broccoli, steamed
handful of blanched fresh peas
handful of fresh chives
1 red [bell] roasted pepper

DRESSING

juice and zest of 1 lemon
1 tbsp extra virgin olive oil
salt and black pepper

OMNIVORE

VEGAN
ALTERNATIVE

*Replace the ham with
a handful of cooked
broad beans*

HAM, TOMATOES, COURGETTI, RADICCHIO & PARSLEY PESTO

INGREDIENTS

*50 g [2 oz] smoked ham
handful of spiralized courgette [zucchini]
6 sun-dried tomatoes, soaked overnight
¼ radicchio, roasted
handful of fresh parsley
handful of pine nuts*

PESTO

*2 tbsp Parsley Pesto (page 119)
1 tbsp extra virgin olive oil
salt and black pepper*

VEGETARIAN

OMNIVORE
ALTERNATIVE
*Add 30 g [1 oz]
fried pancetta*

BLUE CHEESE, ROCKET, CELERIAC & SPELT FETTUCCINE

INGREDIENTS

*100 g [3½ oz] cooked spelt fettuccine
handful of pumpkin seeds
100 g [3½ oz] diced celeriac, roasted
handful of rocket [arugula]
50 g [2 oz] blue cheese, crumbled
sprinkle of fresh thyme*

SAUCE

*1 tbsp tahini
1 tbsp extra virgin olive oil
salt and black pepper*

RAW

PESCATARIAN
ALTERNATIVE
*Add 50 g [2 oz]
poached cod*

CAULIFLOWER, SQUASH, CHIA, CARROT & ALMOND SAUCE

INGREDIENTS

½ purple carrot, ribboned
100 g [3½ oz] raw squash, spiralized
50 g [2 oz] purple cauliflower florets
handful of fresh dill
sprinkle of chia seeds

SAUCE

blend together:
2 tbsp almonds
2 tbsp water
1 tbsp lemon juice
1 tbsp extra virgin olive oil

SALMON, RICE, CUCUMBER, AVOCADO & DULSE

INGREDIENTS

*100 g [3½ oz] cooked brown rice
50 g [2 oz] smoked salmon
handful of spiralized cucumber
½ avocado, sliced
handful of boiled dulse seaweed
sprinkle of sesame seeds*

SAUCE

*2 tbsp extra virgin olive oil
1 tsp tamari soy sauce
salt and black pepper*

EGG, OYSTER MUSHROOMS, ASPARAGUS & BLACK QUINOA

INGREDIENTS

1 hard-boiled egg
handful of oyster mushrooms, fried
100 g [3½ oz] cooked black quinoa
2 asparagus spears, ribboned
handful of fresh parsley

DRESSING

blend together:
1 tbsp extra virgin olive oil
handful of fresh parsley
handful of sunflower seeds, toasted
salt and black pepper

RAW

VEGAN
ALTERNATIVE
*Add 50 g [2 oz]
cooked lentils*

COURGETTI, RED ONION, HEMP, MUSHROOM & SEAWEED

INGREDIENTS

handful of spiralized courgette [zucchini]
½ red onion, thinly sliced
1 portobello mushroom, marinated with
  1 tsp nama shoyu (raw soy sauce)
handful of hemp seeds
sprinkle of red amaranth cress

SAUCE

1 tbsp black sesame tahini
sprinkle of seaweed flakes
1 tbsp extra virgin olive oil
1 tsp nama shoyu (raw soy sauce)

VEGAN

VEGETARIAN ALTERNATIVE

Add 50 g [2 oz] feta cheese

COURGETTI, AUBERGINE, CHICKPEAS & PAPRIKA CREAM

INGREDIENTS

½ *yellow courgette [zucchini], spiralized*
handful of cooked chickpeas
handful of coriander [cilantro]
¼ *aubergine [eggplant], diced and roasted*
½ *red onion, roasted and sliced*
handful of pomegranate seeds

SAUCE

1 tsp paprika
1 tbsp extra virgin olive oil
1 tsp date syrup
1 tsp tahini
salt and black pepper

PESCATARIAN

VEGAN ALTERNATIVE

*Replace the prawns
with a handful of
steamed fresh peas*

PRAWNS, CORN COUSCOUS, MUSHROOMS & TOMATOES

INGREDIENTS

*100 g [3½ oz] cooked corn couscous
handful of cooked Atlantic prawns [shrimp]
handful of fried sliced mushrooms
6 sun-dried tomatoes, soaked overnight
handful of fresh baby coriander [cilantro]
1 spring onion [scallion], sliced*

DRESSING

*2 tbsp extra virgin olive oil
1 tsp lemon juice
sprinkle of sesame seeds
salt and black pepper*

VEGAN

PESCATARIAN ALTERNATIVE

Add 50 g [2 oz] roasted wild salmon or even salmon sashimi

BEANS, CUCUMBER, AVOCADO & SEAWEED SPAGHETTI

INGREDIENTS

handful of cooked kidney beans
100 g [3½ oz] cucumber, spiralized
½ avocado, sliced
handful of seaweed "spaghetti"
sprinkle of sesame seeds, toasted
handful of chives

SAUCE

1 tsp seaweed sprinkle
1 tsp tamari soy sauce
1 tbsp extra virgin olive oil
salt and black pepper

PESCATARIAN

VEGAN ALTERNATIVE

Replace the tuna with cooked edamame beans or broad [fava] beans

TUNA, BLACK NOODLES, AVOCADO & SEAWEED

INGREDIENTS

50g [2 oz] pan-fried tuna, chopped
80 g [2¾ oz] cooked black rice noodles
½ avocado, sliced
¼ red pepper, finely chopped
sprinkle of sesame seeds
handful of fresh chives

SAUCE

1 tsp tamari soy sauce
1 tbsp extra virgin olive oil
sprinkle of nori seaweed
salt and black pepper

OMNIVORE

VEGAN
ALTERNATIVE
*Replace the ham with
a handful of
cooked chickpeas*

HAM, NOODLES, PARSNIP, RED ONION & MUSTARD

INGREDIENTS

*50 g [2 oz] smoked ham
100 g [3½ oz] cooked black rice noodles
1 parsnip, roasted and chopped
1 red onion, roasted and chopped
sprinkle of sesame seeds
handful of fresh parsley*

SAUCE

*1 tbsp mild mustard
1 tbsp extra virgin olive oil
sprinkle of chilli [red pepper] flakes
salt and black pepper*

VEGAN

OMNIVORE
ALTERNATIVE

*Add 50 g [2 oz]
smoked ham or
salt beef*

ROASTED PEPPER, PARSNIP, QUINOA & DULSE

INGREDIENTS

½ roasted red [bell] pepper
¼ red onion, thinly sliced
100 g [3½ oz] cooked quinoa
handful of ribboned parsnip
sprinkle of fresh thyme

DRESSING

1 tbsp extra virgin olive oil
1 tbsp tahini
1 tsp tamari soy sauce
½ tsp dulse seaweed powder
1 tsp sunflower seeds, toasted
salt and black pepper

RAW

VEGETARIAN ALTERNATIVE

Add 50 g [2 oz] shaved pecorino cheese

PARSNIP, GOJI BERRIES, CHILLI & BEETROOT

INGREDIENTS

handful of ribboned raw parsnip
handful of fresh tarragon
handful of sprouted sunflower seeds
1 small beetroot [beet], grated
handful of goji berries, soaked for 10 minutes

SAUCE

1 tbsp extra virgin olive oil
1 tsp lemon juice
1 tsp tahini
sprinkle of chilli powder
salt and black pepper

OMNIVORE

PASTRAMI, BUCKWHEAT, BROCCOLI & CARROT

INGREDIENTS

*50 g [2 oz] pastrami or salt beef
100 g [3½ oz] cooked buckwheat
handful of long-stem broccoli, steamed
½ rainbow carrot, ribboned
sprinkle of fresh thyme*

SAUCE/PÂTÉ

*blend together:
handful of white mushrooms
2 tbsp extra virgin olive oil
1 tbsp tahini
salt and black pepper*

TUNA, NOODLES, BROCCOLI, AVOCADO & PAPRIKA

INGREDIENTS

50 g [2 oz] canned tuna
100 g [3½ oz] cooked rice noodles
2 spring onions [scallions], thinly sliced
handful of broccoli, lightly steamed
½ avocado, sliced
handful of fresh baby coriander [cilantro]

DRESSING

1 tsp smoked paprika
2 tsp extra virgin olive oil
1 tsp lemon juice
1 tsp tahini
sprinkle of black sesame seeds

OMNIVORE

VEGETARIAN ALTERNATIVE

Replace the beef with 50 g [2 oz] feta cheese

SALT BEEF, CORN COUSCOUS, CUCUMBER & POMEGRANATE

INGREDIENTS

50 g [2 oz] salt beef
100 g [3½ oz] cooked corn couscous
handful of spiralized cucumber
handful of pomegranate seeds
handful of fresh tarragon
sprinkle of capers and black sesame seeds

SAUCE

2 tbsp mild mustard
1 tbsp extra virgin olive oil
salt and black pepper

RAW

VEGETARIAN
ALTERNATIVE
*Add 50 g [2 oz]
shaved pecorino cheese*

RADICCHIO, CUCUMBER, TOMATOES & CORIANDER PESTO

INGREDIENTS

handful of shredded radicchio
handful of spiralized cucumber
handful of cherry tomatoes, halved
handful of coriander [cilantro]
sprinkle of pumpkin seeds
sprinkle of sesame seeds

SAUCE

blend together:
handful of fresh coriander [cilantro]
sprinkle of pumpkin seeds
1 tbsp extra virgin olive oil
salt and black pepper

OMNIVORE

VEGAN ALTERNATIVE

Replace the chicken with 2 tbsp cooked black lentils

ROASTED CHICKEN, SUN-DRIED TOMATO, RICE & SQUASH

INGREDIENTS

50 g [2 oz] roasted chicken, sliced
handful of diced roasted butternut squash
100 g [¾ cup] cooked brown rice
6 sun-dried tomatoes, soaked overnight
handful of pumpkin seeds

DRESSING

1 tbsp extra virgin olive oil
1 tbsp tahini
1 tsp lemon juice
salt and black pepper

CHICKEN, COUSCOUS, CUCUMBER & YOGURT

INGREDIENTS

*50 g [2 oz] chicken breast, pan-fried
100 g [3½ oz] cooked couscous
handful of spiralized cucumber
handful of pomegranate seeds
handful of fresh dill
sprinkle of sesame seeds*

SAUCE

*2 tbsp plain yogurt
1 tbsp extra virgin olive oil
salt and black pepper*

VEGAN ALTERNATIVE

Replace the salmon with 50 g [2 oz] cooked black beans

ROASTED SALMON, BROCCOLI, CAULIFLOWER & ONION

INGREDIENTS

50 g [2 oz] honey-roasted salmon
½ small raw cauliflower, blended to "rice"
1 red onion, roasted and sliced
handful of long-stem broccoli florets, steamed
1 tbsp pumpkin seeds, toasted
sprinkle of red amaranth

DRESSING

1 tbsp extra virgin olive oil
1 tbsp tahini
1 tsp tamari soy sauce
sprinkle of nori seaweed
salt and black pepper

VEGAN

OMNIVORE
ALTERNATIVE
*Add 50 g [2 oz]
chorizo*

COURGETTI, BROCCOLI & SMOKED PAPRIKA

INGREDIENTS

*¼ yellow courgette [zucchini], spiralized
handful of blanched long-stem broccoli florets
1 roasted red [bell] pepper
sprinkle of black sesame seeds
sprinkle of red amaranth*

DRESSING

*1 tbsp extra virgin olive oil
1 tsp tahini
1 tsp cider vinegar
1 tsp maple syrup
1 tsp smoked paprika
salt and black pepper*

HAM, CAULIFLOWER, CORN, PEPPER & GUACAMOLE

INGREDIENTS

50 g [2 oz] smoked ham
½ small cauliflower, blended to "rice"
handful of fresh corn kernels
1 roasted red [bell] pepper
handful of fresh tarragon

SAUCE

2 tbsp guacamole
1 tbsp extra virgin olive oil
salt and black pepper

TUNA, MILLET, RADICCHIO, RED ONION & MUSTARD

INGREDIENTS

50 g [2 oz] canned tuna
100 g [3½ oz] cooked millet
handful of radicchio, shredded
¼ red onion, thinly sliced
handful of pumpkin seeds, toasted
handful of fresh parsley

SAUCE

1 tsp mild mustard
1 tbsp extra virgin olive oil
1 tsp lemon juice
salt and black pepper

BRESAOLA, COURGETTI, TOMATOES & PARMESAN

INGREDIENTS

*30 g [1 oz] cured bresaola beef
handful of spiralized courgette [zucchini]
handful of cherry tomatoes, quartered
30 g [1 oz] shaved Parmesan cheese
handful of pea shoots or rocket [arugula]
handful of fresh parsley*

DRESSING

*1 tbsp extra virgin olive oil
1 tsp lemon juice
salt and black pepper*

VEGAN

PESCATARIAN
ALTERNATIVE

*Add 50 g [2 oz]
smoked mackerel*

PARSNIP, BROCCOLI, HEMP & POMEGRANATE

INGREDIENTS

1 tbsp shelled hemp seeds
1 small parsnip, ribboned
handful of blanched long-stem broccoli florets
handful of pomegranate seeds
handful of fresh chives

DRESSING

1 tbsp extra virgin olive oil
1 tbsp tahini
1 tbsp ground turmeric
salt and black pepper

CARROT, CAULIFLOWER, QUINOA & SCAMORZA CREAM

INGREDIENTS

1 carrot, chopped and roasted
100 g [3½ oz] cauliflower florets, roasted
100 g [3½ oz] cooked black quinoa
sprinkle of fresh thyme

CREAM

melt together:
2 tbsp single [light] cream
2 tbsp scamorza cheese

OMNIVORE

VEGETARIAN
ALTERNATIVE
*Replace the chicken
with a soft-boiled egg*

ROASTED CHICKEN, AVOCADO, CARROT & BUCKWHEAT

INGREDIENTS

*100 g [3½ oz] cooked buckwheat
1 carrot, ribboned and roasted
½ avocado, sliced
50 g [2 oz] roasted chicken
handful of fresh coriander [cilantro]
1 tbsp toasted pumpkin seeds*

DRESSING

*1½ tbsp olive oil
1 tsp tahini
1 tsp cider vinegar
1 tsp maple syrup
1 tsp smoked paprika*

PESCATARIAN

VEGETARIAN ALTERNATIVE

Replace the prawns with 50 g [2 oz] halloumi cheese

PRAWNS, PEPPER, AUBERGINE, PURPLE KALE & BASIL

INGREDIENTS

*1 roasted red [bell] pepper, sliced
handful of purple kale, steamed
1 spring onion [scallion], finely chopped
handful of cooked Atlantic prawns [shrimp]
¼ aubergine [eggplant], diced and roasted
sprinkle of fresh basil*

DRESSING

*½ tbsp lemon juice
1 tbsp of extra virgin olive oil
salt and black pepper*

VEGAN

PESCATARIAN ALTERNATIVE

Add 50 g [2 oz] roasted wild salmon

RICE, AUBERGINE, TOMATOES, PEAS & TAHINI LEMON CREAM

INGREDIENTS

handful of fresh peas
100 g [3½ oz] cooked jasmine rice
¼ aubergine [eggplant], diced and roasted
handful of cherry tomatoes, halved
handful of coriander [cilantro]

SAUCE

1 tsp tahini
1 tbsp extra virgin olive oil
1 tsp lemon juice
sprinkle of chilli [red pepper] flakes
sprinkle of black sesame seeds

SCAMORZA, ASPARAGUS, BUCKWHEAT & HUMMUS

INGREDIENTS

50 g [2 oz] smoked scamorza cheese, chopped
100 g [3½ oz] cooked buckwheat
3 asparagus spears, roasted
handful of fresh tarragon
½ carrot, ribboned
dash of extra virgin olive oil

HUMMUS

blend together:
1 tbsp extra virgin olive oil
140g [1 cup] cooked chickpeas
1 tbsp lemon juice
1 tsp tahini
salt and black pepper

PESCATARIAN ALTERNATIVE

Add 50 g [2 oz] roasted wild salmon

PINE NUTS, COURGETTI, CHILLI, CAVOLO NERO & TOMATOES

INGREDIENTS

handful of pine nuts
1 small courgette [zucchini], spiralized
handful of cavolo nero, chopped and
   massaged with lemon juice
handful of cherry tomatoes, halved
handful of fresh parsley

SAUCE

1 tbsp lemon juice
sprinkle of chilli [red pepper] flakes
1 tbsp extra virgin olive oil
1 tsp tahini
salt and black pepper

PRAWNS, COURGETTE, BARLEY & SAFFRON

INGREDIENTS

handful of cooked Atlantic prawns [shrimps]
100 g [3½ oz] cooked pearl barley
1 onion, roasted and sliced
½ courgette [zucchini], roasted and sliced
handful of fresh parsley

DRESSING

1 tbsp extra virgin olive oil
pinch of saffron threads
salt and black pepper

VEGAN
ALTERNATIVE
*Replace the cream
with oat or soy cream*

TAGLIATELLE, PEPPER, BLACK PEAS, RADICCHIO & CREAM

INGREDIENTS

handful of cooked black/carlin peas
handful of radicchio, roasted
a few fresh chives
1 roasted red [bell] pepper, sliced
100 g [3½ oz] cooked spelt tagliatelle

CREAM

3 tbsp single [light] cream
drizzle of olive oil
salt and black pepper
sprinkle of saffron threads

OMNIVORE

VEGAN ALTERNATIVE

Replace the chicken with 2 tbsp cooked black lentils

SMOKED HAM, JERUSALEM ARTICHOKE, KALE & YOGURT

INGREDIENTS

50 g [2 oz] smoked ham
handful of purple kale, lightly steamed
100 g [3½ oz] Jerusalem artichokes, roasted
handful of pomegranate seeds
sprinkle of sesame seeds
sprinkle of fresh thyme

SAUCE

1 tbsp plain yogurt
1 tbsp Dijon mustard
1 tbsp extra virgin olive oil
salt and black pepper

RAW

VEGETARIAN ALTERNATIVE

Replace the coconut yogurt with Greek yogurt

CUCUMBER, GOJI BERRIES & COCONUT YOGURT

INGREDIENTS

handful of spiralized cucumber
2 radishes, sliced
handful of goji berries, soaked in water for
  15 minutes
½ pink grapefruit, chopped
sprinkle of black sesame seeds and cress

DRESSING

1 tbsp extra virgin olive oil
1 tbsp coconut yogurt
salt and black pepper

VEGETARIAN

OMNIVORE ALTERNATIVE

Replace the feta cheese with 50 g [2 oz] salt beef

FETA, RICE, CAULIFLOWER, POMEGRANATE & TAHINI

INGREDIENTS

50 g [2 oz] feta cheese, crumbled
100 g [3½ oz] cooked brown rice
100 g [3½ oz] cooked mung beans
handful of cauliflower florets, roasted
handful of pomegranate seeds
handful of fresh tarragon

DRESSING

1 tbsp tahini
1 tbsp extra virgin olive oil
salt and black pepper

CHICKEN, RICE, SQUASH, BROCCOLI & PESTO

INGREDIENTS

50 g [2 oz] fried chicken breast pieces
100 g [3½ oz] cooked white rice
100 g [3½ oz] squash, roasted
handful of broccoli, steamed
handful of fresh basil
handful of pine nuts

PESTO

1 tbsp classic pesto
1 tbsp extra virgin olive oil
salt and black pepper

COD, QUINOA, RED PEPPER & OLIVES

INGREDIENTS

*50 g [2 oz] roasted cod fillet
100 g [3 oz] cooked black quinoa
½ roasted red [bell] pepper
handful of green olives
sprinkle of pine nuts
handful of fresh parsley*

SAUCE

*1 tsp lemon juice
1 tbsp extra virgin olive oil
salt and black pepper*

EGG, SPINACH, MUSHROOMS, PASTA & MUSTARD CREAM

INGREDIENTS

*1 soft-boiled egg
2 portobello mushrooms, roasted
handful of spinach, quickly fried
100 g [3½ oz] cooked spelt farfalle pasta
handful of fresh tarragon
sprinkle of poppy seeds*

CREAM

*2 tbsp single [light] cream
1 tbsp mild mustard
drizzle of olive oil
salt and black pepper*

INDEX

ACKNOWLEDGMENTS

*I would like to thank my wife for the unlimited patience and support she gives me,
even when I do things that apparently don't make sense.*

Thank you to my son who displays sensitivity and purity every day.

Thank you to my dad who is always there to support and guide me.

Thank you to my aunty and uncle who have adopted me like a son.

Thank you to my extended family for showing passion and generosity every day.

Thank you to my editor Céline and my agent Claudia for incredible patience and advice.

*Thanks to all the people I've worked with during my time as a graphic designer,
as you all supported me and my crazy choices so much.*

Thanks to all my friends who help me to be strong and humble.

Thanks to all the people who helped me with my crowdfunding campaign that made my dream true.

*Thanks to all the people I've worked with and I currently work with in Neal's Yard;
you helped me so much.*

Thank you, Mum, for always being there like the North Star.